Meditatio
Mindfulness for A Hectic Life
How to Reduce Stress and Create a Happier You

Simple, practical techniques you can use even while boiling the kettle!

H. Z. Rose

HAPPY AND CALM

Contents

Introduction - Why I decided to write this book

Are you overwhelmed, stressed, or anxious?

Well, my hope is that this will be one of the best reads you have picked up in a while! This book will provide you with some simple tools for making small changes that can make a huge difference and create a calmer and happier you.

I am really excited that you have chosen to take a chance and give this a shot – so thank you. Plus, it means someone has actually purchased (or downloaded) a copy, so I'm not just talking to myself!

My promise: This will be a no-waffle, practical pick-up book that you can use straight away. I have no intention of droning on for twenty pages, telling you how great meditation and mindfulness is. I'm sure you already know about the potential benefits.

My aim: To provide lots of simple ways for you to apply basic meditation and mindfulness techniques to the most mundane of tasks in your life. And I will show you how to make these techniques work for you in the real world.

My life (like millions of you out there!) is super hectic. Trying to remember to do everything for everyone is a constant juggling act – one that I feel I never succeed at. By pleasing one person, I seem to neglect another. The saying "you can't please everyone" sometimes feels so true. The never-ending "to-do" list – remembering to bleach the toilet, buy the "right" food for packed lunches they will actually eat, feed my family with enough fruit and vegetables so that they are not vitamin-deficient. Not to mention work demands and the necessity to run the vacuum around the house and keep some semblance of a clean home.

Then, trawling through the calendar to try and squeeze in the occasional date night and break the daily monotony. Oh, and actually trying to find time for **me** among the chaos – which everyone tells me is "sooo" important now.

Have I missed anything?

The demands of modern life are very challenging and pressurized – now more than ever. I have spent years struggling to do it all for everyone: my children, my husband, my work. But frequently, I felt like it wasn't quite good enough. Like I was not quite good enough. Finally (after many years, I might add), it feels like I have hit a point in my life where I am more in control and in a calmer place. However, don't be fooled! I'm not saying that I feel permanently in control—and particularly not when my two children are yet again screaming at each other over how many cookies the other one has eaten and about how unfair life is!

So what changed for me? The answer: **Meditation and Mindfulness**. It has totally changed my perspective and outlook.

Firstly, don't panic. I am not suggesting that you should sit on a squishy yoga mat in a quiet, Zen-like state for thirty minutes a day, stretching your limbs into what appears to be an impossible position (especially past a certain age). You are awesome if you're one of those amazing people – and if you are, then I can promise this book will provide some welcome additions to your routine (and requires no additional flexibility!).

However, if, like me, you lack the necessary flexibility, then rest assured that the next thirty pages can be practiced anywhere, at any time, and require no stretching whatsoever!

When my two children were very little, it was nearly impossible to find time to do anything for *me* – and I'm sure this will resonate with many of you. Even having a quick pee was frequently interrupted, and at times it felt like there was no escape space in the house. There always seemed to be something else that needed doing or demands from others such as my family, friends, or work to fit in. And my needs fell to the back of the line.

Trust me. You will be able to fit my suggestions into your day – even among the yells of "What are we having for dinner?"

and between driving the kids here and there as their glorified taxi driver. Even in the busiest of schedules.

How? This is real-life meditation and mindfulness. And the beauty is that you can fit it in around the ordinary and essential things you have to do, like having a shower or bath, chopping the vegetables and even ironing!

I searched for a modern approach and found nothing that worked with my hectic life. So now, I am sharing what worked for me and is still working on a daily basis. I will provide you with easy, practical ideas that you can pick up and use straight away.

I am so excited to share what I have learned on my own journey – and I hope my experiences provide some ideas that you can implement yourself.

Soon you will have the tools to be a calmer and happier version of yourself.

Thank you, and good luck.

My background

Everyone who knows me comments that I am always on the go. I like being busy. In fact, I thrive on it. But sometimes, I am my own worst enemy and don't know when to stop. I work full-time as a teacher, have two children, a husband, a cat, and a hamster, plus an online business that I started a few years ago (because clearly, I didn't have enough to do and had far too much spare time on my hands!). Life is very much hectic, but I love it that way – most of the time! However, in order to manage it all, I can't do it without help.

> *in order to manage it all I can't do it without help*

That's where meditation and mindfulness come in. They have been part of my life for years in many different guises – from visiting a Buddhist meditation center as part of my bachelor's degree to practicing breathing meditation in class with my students to help calm their exam nerves. I have always been consciously aware of their benefits. My students would come and chat with me and tell me how these had really helped get them through their exams and how they had been using them at home. It felt good, knowing I had made a difference in their lives. And I have shared the technique with hundreds of young people over my many years of teaching.

However, it was not until I personally felt the impact that it really made me appreciate and realize the benefits of what meditation and mindfulness can offer.

It all started many years ago when I began trying to find a "cure" to manage my anxiety attacks. They were triggered by my experiences growing up, and they had decided to suddenly re-appear as my stress levels had recently risen.

It occurred to me that I had never truly dealt with them. And now, as an adult, they had surfaced again – leaving me feeling totally out of control. My heart would just start pounding, and then I'd lose the ability to breathe and would feel so out of control, which just made the whole thing worse and left me powerless to do anything.

For weeks it plagued the back of my mind. I kept thinking that they would disappear, but after one particularly frightening episode, I finally got the courage to do something about it.

That was when I started looking into spiritual practices, and the most obvious one was, of course, yoga. But I didn't have the time for a weekly yoga class. I barely had time for everything else that had to be done on a daily basis and just didn't feel I could commit. Plus, deep down, I knew my heart wasn't in it. I knew that any good intentions wouldn't last long and that I would do my usual thing after the novelty had worn off – come up with excuses not to turn up.

As a natural result, my second option was meditation. I don't have twenty or thirty minutes a day to sit quietly in one spot, trying to focus my mind on gaining more clarity and peace. The demands of family and work-life just do not lend themselves to this, and there is no corner of my house where I can't be found! However, I just felt that this was the one for me and was determined to make it work.

So my journey began, and everything slowly began to click into place. I started to use meditation mindfulness throughout the day, whenever I remembered—when I was stuck in traffic or hanging the washing out—and it became a sort of "meditation-on-the-go." I just made up the term to cope with my timeframe, and it worked. Some days, I managed it three times, other days not at all. But gradually, over time, I incorporated it more and more into my daily routine.

> *Mum, you are so much calmer.*

The epiphany came one morning when my children commented, "Mum, you are so much calmer in the morning now. You don't shout anymore." I think that said it all. Without much additional effort, I did feel different, calmer, and less stressed. It had just gradually crept up on me, and I hadn't even realized it myself.

You can adapt it to suit your needs

My meditation has changed and adapted throughout the years as my children have grown. To begin with, my intended daily plan was very simple: get up every morning stupidly early (before the children move), and use this time to write my targets for the day and do 5-10 minutes of breathing meditation before my work. I am not suggesting you do this, but this is what I planned would work for me.

I have no doubt that if I had an active social media account and snapped every inch of my life, the following perfect photo would be staged: a trendy image of my funky journal (with a positive affirmation on it, of course) and a very posh pen alongside a steaming latte bearing a pretty picture created from one of those elaborate stencils. Sure to make everyone else feel completely inadequate as they crawl out of bed, and to give the impression that my life is amazing and super perfect.

Now for a reality check, which is not often snapped! Instead of the above, my youngest got up and proceeded to talk at me without taking a break for air for what felt like forever (this was 5.15 am)!! I know. My gentle suggestions of, "it's very early, do you not want to try and go back to bed?" fell on deaf ears. My brain went into overdrive, thinking, "I get up this early to have this time to myself. Is it too much to have 10 minutes in a morning!" I realized there was no point fighting it or getting overly annoyed – it wasn't going to happen. Most mornings recently, the shower is my chosen place for mindfulness, and this works for me. Does it matter? No, not at all. There is no point in trying to achieve the "ideal" time and place. It will never happen. Do what works for you. Life is full of interruptions.

It could be morning, at work, at night. You could forget one day or not feel like doing it. That is life, and we put too much pressure on ourselves. Even if you manage three days out of seven at first, just do what works for you and your situation. We are all different and have different demands put on us.

I promise, nothing is ever easy when you try to perfect it. Perfection in itself is impossible and, with a hectic life, we are resorting to meditation to make life simpler and less stressful.

If you have a one-hour lunch break at work, take ten minutes of it to sit calmly (even at your desk if there is nowhere else to go), close your eyes, and focus on your breath as you inhale and exhale. Even just a few minutes daily will be worth it – and that, too, is a promise. I have even sat in the bathroom at work for a little peace. Do whatever works!

So, is this meditation? Well, it is, but not in its most perfect form as written in countless other books. But remember, we are not seeking perfection here. In fact, we're trying to avoid perfect as—in such a fast-paced life with responsibilities so numerous that they start to blur into each other—perfect is the enemy.

Whether you're dealing with children, a demanding job, or an impossible study schedule, remember that you chose this book because you want to find calm inside of yourself so that you can face the demands of your day. Keep your mind's eye on that goal, and that goal only.

As you can see, even my plan of waking up at the break of dawn to get my ten minutes of meditation didn't work because it seems that, like all children, mine have sensors telling them when I'm up and ready to interact (in their opinion).

I don't let the minor or major setbacks get to me. Well, most of the time, I don't. Some days, it just doesn't happen, and the best thing is to accept that this is okay too. Move on and try tomorrow or when you jump into bed that night if you are not too exhausted to stay awake for a few minutes.

How does this book work?

This book will guide you step by step while you find the right meditation style that suits **your** needs and **your** everyday schedule.

After you are familiar with different types of meditation, we'll move into how to practice meditation and mindfulness in different settings and how to adjust to get the right set-up for you. This is not an exhaustive list and doesn't cover every possible example, but instead gives ideas and suggestions that you can pick up and adapt to your needs. It is more a guide to give you the confidence to try out different things that will work for your life.

Lastly, I will include my personal tips for you to reach a happier version of yourself.

Why is meditation good for you?

In my opinion, there is no denying how important meditation is. To truly benefit from any activity you choose to do, you must be aware of the potential benefits this activity can bring you so that you're willing to give it a good attempt.

I was fortunate that through my studies and teaching work, I had witnessed first-hand the benefits of meditation and mindfulness for my students. It seemed a natural progression to be able to now harness this and use it to help me in my life.

So what are the benefits? Countless research projects highlight the positives of using mindfulness meditation for reducing stress and controlling anxiety.

What about the long-term and medical-related benefits?

It isn't a surprise to learn that meditation helps with insomnia, high blood pressure, short attention span, and in the long run, can prevent heart disease. Stress and anxiety directly affect our sleep patterns, so anything that can offer a better night's sleep is a winner.

> *meditation helps to control pain*

What I was surprised to learn is that meditation helps to control pain, especially for people suffering from a chronic condition.

If you're as shocked as I was when I learned this, let me walk you through the logic behind it.

A study conducted back in 2012, including 47 trials with more than 3500 participants, found that mindfulness meditation improved cases of anxiety, depression, and pain.

The simple explanation for this study's findings is that each person's perception of pain depends on their state of mind when the pain is happening. Since mindfulness meditation improves the individual's self-awareness, it ultimately helps the person to reach the level of calmness and acceptance that shifts their state of mind in a more positive direction, which helps with the pain.

In other words, a person who is experiencing pain while being stressed about work (for example) feels the pain in a more elevated way than another person who is experiencing the same level of pain while sitting in a garden on a sunny day with nothing to worry about. I mean, how amazing is that!

Regularly practicing mindfulness meditation helps you to get in that "sitting in a garden on a sunny day" state of mind, which helps you to control the pain.

A perfect example of this is when I went into hospital for my second hip operation. The anesthetist couldn't locate the correct part of my spine to inject. I know, it was painful! Despite me stating it had been an issue last time, the doctor just nodded and said there was nothing in my notes (so clearly, it mustn't have happened)! Visualization and breathing meditation was a Godsend and honestly got me through as she stabbed me numerous times along my spine, trying to find the correct place. So, I can personally vouch that this worked for me. She apologized profusely later (when I was half-conscious) – apparently, I have the spine of a small child (so, of course, it was my fault). She did say she felt awful (and she looked terribly guilty). However, it proved you can use these techniques anywhere, even when you are sat in a freezing cold theater wearing a surgical gown while perched on a metal bed being stared at by a full surgical team!

In a nutshell, mindfulness meditation essentially improves your emotional and mental health, which gives your entire body the chance to cope with pain, get better, and maintain a healthier state. What's not to love about this?

Different types of meditation

During my search to find the best type of meditation to suit my everyday schedule, I came across 5 main types, which, most of the time, overlap. In this section of the book, I'm going to introduce and explain all 5 types so that you can familiarize yourself and perhaps identify a favorite one, or favorite combination, before we get started with the practical steps to start your meditation routine.

Remember, the goal of this whole process is to reduce your anxiety and stress. So, there is no need to restrict yourself to a specific practice. If you choose one type of meditation and then find that it's not the one for you, it is perfectly fine to come back to this book, try a different one, or combine different types.

Keep this process as light and fun as you possibly can to eliminate the risk of adding any more burdens and reasons for anxiety in your life.

Let's begin!

Spoken Meditation (Guided Meditation)

I'm starting with this type of meditation because it is one of the most popular styles of meditation for beginners.

Spoken meditation, or guided meditation, depends on having a meditation teacher —usually a trained person who is experienced in meditation. This person will guide the participant (that's you) through a series of instructions that aim to help you clear your mind, increase your self-awareness, and enter a meditative state.

Spoken or guided meditation is available on many platforms, such as YouTube videos. You can also find dedicated apps. If you'd like to give it a go but don't feel that you have the time, it would be a good idea to try it right before bedtime. When lying in bed, get your earphones ready, and play a video or start the app. There are some useful links on my website: www.happyandcalm.com.

Breathing Mindfulness Meditation

The second type is another beginner-friendly meditation, and it requires only that you focus the entirety of your attention on your breathing. There is nothing more to it than focusing on the inhales and exhales as you breathe in a rhythmic pattern. There are lots of different breathing techniques to choose from.

The box breathing style is an easy starter which focuses on breathing in slowly through your nose, holding your breath for a few seconds (as long as is comfortable), then exhaling slowly from your mouth, and repeating.

As you might have guessed, this is my favorite type of meditation as it can be done at any time and in any place, and it doesn't require any specific setting or circumstance. It is amazing how such a simple process can re-focus and calm the mind.

As we progress through this book's chapters, breathing mindfulness meditation is going to be the type I refer to most, as it is the perfect type for a hectic life!

Movement Meditation

This type is also known as meditative movement. As the name indicates, it uses body movements in specific positions to get into a meditative state and gain the needed calmness, relaxation, and clarity of mind.

Yoga is the most famous form of movement meditation. So, if you like yoga, then you've already found your style!

Visualization Meditation

Visualization meditation depends on visualizing something in particular – for example, a place where you feel safe and content. Even if that place doesn't exist in reality, as long as it helps you to relax, it will be perfect for staying in your mind during your visualization meditation.

You can also visualize an event, an object, or even a loved one who will help you feel loved, relaxed, and help the stress melt away.

I often visualize my ideal picture postcard, which involves a beautiful white sandy beach, clear, sparkling, blue warm waters lapping at my feet, my children playing in the shallow water with my husband laughing as I relax on a padded sun lounger sipping a cocktail. If only! Yes, that is why it's just a visualization – but it does do the job of relaxing me and taking me to my "happy place."

This type of meditation often overlaps with guided meditation or spoken meditation as the teacher or the person leading your meditation will guide you to your visualization of choice.

Chanting Meditation

Many studies have found that sounds can have relaxing and even healing effects. In this type of meditation, the sound of chanting is used to change consciousness and help the participant enter a deeper state of meditation.

While this specific type may seem too advanced or complicated, thanks to technology, you can now get a similar experience by meditating using lo-fi music, which will help you to enter the desired meditative state.

This music can be found abundantly (and for free) on YouTube. So, it's low cost and, just like guided or spoken meditation, it will only require a set of headphones

Chapter 1 - Everyday Essentials

I've lost count of the essential activities I do each day. I mean, how many times do you boil the kettle, have a drink, or eat something?

We all know time is precious. We all already have too many things to do. The perfect solution is to incorporate mindfulness meditation into the things we already do on a daily basis. You can get your relaxation hit without having to set aside a designated time of the day.

In this chapter, I'm going to go through several activities that almost every person does every day to guide you through the ways I found to perfectly incorporate mindfulness meditation into these everyday essentials.

Boiling the Kettle

Clicking the kettle on can be the ideal opportunity to take some time to practice mindfulness. Whether it's the first thing you do in the morning, or you're waiting for your kettle to boil later in the day, this time is the perfect opportunity to start your mindfulness practice.

Try sitting at the kitchen table or standing by the kettle and start to slowly inhale for four counts through your nose and exhale for four counts through your mouth.

This is all I do. I don't close my eyes because I might actually nod off (especially if it is later in the afternoon), but feel free to do so if this helps you focus.

If you have to keep your eyes open for any reason (like me), then just focus your consciousness on the breathing and clear your mind as much as you can by counting the breaths. Feel your chest rise and fall. Feel the warm air in your mouth and nose. Or use the box technique I described earlier.

Don't push yourself or feel the pressure to be 100% clear-minded from the first moment or the first day.

It's okay if you zone out or get distracted. Just calmly bring your focus back to the rhythmic breathing and keep going.

If you're able to focus for even 30 seconds or 1 minute for the first time, this would be a great result. It's not as easy as you think to just "clear your mind," so anything you can manage is a bonus.

> *anything you can manage is a bonus*

With time, you'll find yourself better able to focus. You will be able to clear and calm your mind for 5 minutes (or whatever length of time works for you). The important thing is to keep trying, don't put pressure on your mind, avoid increasing the stress, and take it one second at a time.

If you prefer a more visual aid, try and focus on the kettle itself as you breathe deeply: the steam rising, the vibrations, and the noise. It really is a case of trying it and seeing what works best for you. There is no right or wrong.

Peeling and Chopping Vegetables

When it comes to everyday meals, I try to keep myself and my family healthy. Whether I'm cooking dinner or preparing lunch boxes, I always try to include some sort of fruit and vegetables.

How about making the most of this time by being mindful?

Obviously, I don't close my eyes (as I want to keep my fingers, thank you), nor do I focus all my attention on counting my breaths.

I have to be focused on the task at hand. I give 100% of my attention to what my hands are doing, and this can be used as the focus. I follow the knife's movements up and down on the cutting board and notice the little pieces of vegetable forming.

Being mindful is to be present in the moment, and that is exactly what I do during meal preparations. I'm present with my consciousness in my current time and place. I'm here with my knife, cutting board, and vegetables. And that's it.

I don't let my mind wander to other issues. I block out any other thoughts about anything else – whether it's as big as a problem at work or as small as the task I need to do next. Try and bring your breathing in time with each chop, and focus on letting your whole body relax.

I also try to keep my breathing rhythmic. But—unlike the time when I'm boiling the kettle—I don't put all of my focus into it. I just remember to breathe calmly, inhale through the nose, and exhale through the mouth. And it's as simple as that.

Eating & Drinking

Another time for mindfulness to take a new form is when you are eating and drinking.

Let me tell you first of all that I find food to be one of life's greatest joys. In such a busy life, sitting down to have a tasty meal is the point in my day that I love the most. Thankfully, I am now in the fortunate position where I actually get my food while it's still hot. I vividly remember furiously chopping various items on everyone else's plates before I could settle and grab a bit of lukewarm (at best) food for myself.

Being mindful while eating has not only helped me to enjoy my meals even more, but it also helps to avoid problems with digestion and eating too quickly.

Too often, I would sit at the table with my mind already busy with everything that I had to do, not only after dinner but the next day too! I didn't focus on what I was eating or drinking, and I ended up eating as fast as possible just to get it out the way so I could get on with my other jobs.

This pattern of thinking and speed meant I never really tasted anything I put in my mouth. Needless to say, I would end up feeling hungry a short time after I'd eaten a full meal because I didn't pay attention to what I'd just consumed. This then led to a sneaky walk to the snack cupboard most evenings, where I would munch on a variety of items that would leave me bloated at bedtime and would often mean I'd wake up with indigestion the next day. I would then feel very guilty, and with a solemn vow, I would promise I would be better today. Well, some days I managed it...

Once I started practicing mindfulness during my eating time, I started noticing a difference right away. I wasn't hungry just one hour after I finished eating. I didn't need to eat right after my big meals. And, as a natural result, indigestion was on its way out of my life. Take the time and see if you can follow any of the tips below.

Here's how mindfulness can improve your eating time:

•**Do not eat on the run**. When it is time to eat, sit at a table. It's only a few minutes.

•**Keep your mind completely focused** on the food you're eating. Concentrate on your hands' movements, and the bites, the flavors, the textures in your mouth right now.

•**Take your time chewing**. Experts recommend 24 to 30 seconds of chewing for every bite, but we know that's not possible here. So, at least don't swallow your food almost whole (as I used to do to get it done). Chew for a few seconds. This will help you enjoy the meal more, and you will feel full sooner and for a longer time.

•**Keep your mind busy** with the plates, the colors of the food, the different flavors, and so on. Keep anything other than the food you're eating out of your mind.

Commuting/Traveling

This particular point depends on whether you drive to work, get driven to work by a friend, or travel on public transport.

If you drive to work, then the setting won't be suitable for you to focus your attention on one single thing, as you must be alert and focusing on driving.

However, this is a great opportunity to benefit from one of mindfulness's biggest gifts: calmness.

If you manage to achieve self-awareness by practicing mindfulness (remember, this is just being in the moment with

all of your consciousness), then you can keep yourself calm, even when other drivers aren't following the rules of the road.

If you're not driving yourself to work, then this is a golden opportunity. You can use this precious time to close your eyes, get into your mindfulness meditation state, and start relaxing before your workday even starts!

This technique has helped me in a massive way on days when I've had important meetings or presentations at work. Instead of spending my journey to work worrying about my day and then arriving riddled with anxiety and exhausted from over-thinking every single detail, I would get into a calm state, which made me confident and able to focus on every detail in turn. Try and use this time to focus on your breathing and to visualize all that is good in your life. Or imagine your ideal day. Thinking positive thoughts really can make it happen

Chapter 2 - Making the Mundane Useful

In this chapter, I decided to cover the most mundane and tedious activities that we all have to suffer through every day and every week. With mindfulness, not only are these chores and activities transformed into something I benefit from, but with time, I have come to enjoy doing them!

Laundry Tasks

In the past, I thought that you'd have to be some kind of a saint not to hate everything about laundry. It is, by far, one of the house's most boring and time-consuming responsibilities. And it seems to be never-ending.

However, thanks to mindfulness meditation, it turned out to be just what I needed. It gave me the time to practice and, eventually, relax.

You see, when my mind was cluttered, and I had a million things to worry about, spending my time hanging and folding laundry seemed almost like torture. My mind would be going on and on about what was going wrong in life, about all the things I needed to do, and all the while, I was stuck sorting out the clothes!

Now, with mindfulness, I can clear my mind. And—although I still have a million and one things that need to be done—training my mind to exist in the moment has helped me to stop the stress of over-thinking about what isn't here now.

Sorting clothes, folding them into piles, the repeated actions are an ideal environment in which to practice your breathing. As you fold the clothes, use the movements of folding to relax by rotating your shoulders, turning your head slowly while breathing, and counting your breaths.

Washing Dishes, Vacuuming, Ironing

Believe it or not, washing the dishes can become one of your favorite things too! I know, you don't believe me.

With time, washing the dishes becomes a mechanical movement that your body does without your mind having to do much. As a natural result, your mind starts to wander to other things. Maybe some of these things are stress-inducing. Maybe you start thinking about something that happened at work, and you replay the incident in your head. As the minutes go by, you start feeling angry again and, before you know it, you're consumed by some form of negative feeling – whether it is stress, anger, or sorrow.

With the right practice of mindful meditation while washing the dishes, you can stop this negative train of thought before it begins.

Once you start the dishes, begin breathing in slow, deep breaths. Focus on your breaths. And then, once you get the rhythm, start focusing your thoughts on what's in your hands. Is it the foamy soap? Is it the warm water running down to clear away all the spots and impurities from your shiny dishes?

Enjoy the process as the pile of dirty dishes shrinks, and the pile of squeaky-clean dishes grows. Use this time to practice your breathing as you focus on cleaning the dishes.

This exercise will both help you to gain clarity and become relaxed as well as to gain a sense of accomplishment as you see the progress of your labor with a conscious mind. In time, doing the dishes will increase your appreciation of yourself.

The same method can be applied to all chores and all housework that require automatic repetitive movements such as ironing clothes and vacuuming.

Self-care

Do you work out? I'm going to be completely honest with you. I rarely work out. It just isn't for me (especially with my inadequate hips), and I just don't enjoy it at all. I was also too stressed and too busy to even think about setting aside time to take care of myself in any way.

I'm not claiming that mindfulness miraculously created more time in the day. Of course not. But when I started to control my stress and anxiety levels, I was less tired and less consumed by every thought that went through my head. As a result, I had the emotional capacity to start taking care of myself. And now I regularly head out for walks along the coast where I live.

Your skincare routine could be another ideal opportunity to focus and take time to visualize and breathe as you cleanse, tone, and moisturize. It can ease your stress and reduce dark circles and acne, thus benefitting your skin if you practice this on a daily basis. You might as well make the most of the time.

This got me thinking about my body. If you prefer more active meditation, yoga is the perfect option, and there are countless YouTube videos. Maybe select a few favorite moves and implement these around your daily activities. Yoga is a perfect option if you prefer more movement, and it is a spiritual practice that can be directly connected to mindfulness.

This is not to say that you can't run (for example) or do any other kind of exercise. As long as you remember to clear your mind, organize your breathing, and focus on the "here & now," exercise will be the perfect meditative practice

Chapter 3 - The Outdoors

Life's responsibilities must go on, and so must your journey with mindfulness. In this chapter, we're moving on to activities that you probably do less often. Once again, practicing mindfulness can help you turn the time spent on these tasks into something productive and relaxing.

Mowing the Grass

Just like with vacuuming, mowing the grass is a repetitive task that requires a somewhat automatic motion. Your mindfulness practice here is going to be more enjoyable than vacuuming, however, thanks to the lovely smell of freshly cut grass, seeing the progress in the grass's shape and color, and creating lines as you mow. As you move, you can practice a combination of breathing and movement and also get something else off your "to do" list.

Weeding

This is one of the most suitable activities for practicing mindfulness. As you weed your yard or garden, being mindful will help you push away other thoughts as your fingers sink deeper into the soil, paying attention to the location of the weeds and the method you're using to remove them. It is often the ideal task for allowing your mind to wander off and focus on the positives in life and to appreciate the nature around you.

Walking

Walking and taking in nature has enormous benefits. Not only do you feel the fresh air on your skin as you walk, but you can also zone out to a large extent and really focus on your box breathing, think of the positives in your life, think of the things you would like to achieve.

In such cases, mindfulness meditation will help you embrace walking and enjoy your time while doing it. You can even incorporate coffee and cake on the route back, so it gives you even more incentive!

Washing the Car

Practicing mindfulness while washing the car can be similar to your activity when washing the dishes, with the added value of being outside where you can enjoy the weather and fresh air. So spend your time with a clear head thinking about the shining sun (although this is unlikely if you are in the UK like me) while enjoying the result of your labor as your car becomes as good-looking as new.

For me, I've got to confess that the car washing is left to my husband, but he uses this time to listen to calming music or positive audiobooks – so do whatever works for you, whatever helps you relax.

Chapter 4 - Creative

Getting creative with your meditation time can definitely make it more enjoyable, especially when you're just getting started. When you have a vast imagination and a restless mind, it is super easy for your mind to wander to other thoughts, spaces, and even worlds(!). So, even if you succeed at clearing your mind of stress-related thoughts, it is also important to stop it from running wild. After all, mastering mindfulness meditation depends on keeping your awareness in the "here and now." So, it would be counterproductive if you finished your meditation only to realize that you had spent the entire time in Narnia!

In this chapter, I have outlined some of the most popular items (including my own personal favorite – reading) to use creatively during your meditation time.

Candles

There are multiple ways to utilize candles in your meditation, and I am a huge fan of using them. Depending on your preference, you can purchase an array of scented candles that can help you relax – choose lavender, citrus, or peppermint, depending on the ambiance you want to create. Associating the pleasant smell of the candle with your mindfulness experience will deepen your attachment to the practice, and you will like it more quickly and get used to it faster. The combination of breathing and the smell can really heighten the experience.

You can also stare at the candle flame while you're entering a meditative state. Focus solely on it. The flame is famous for helping people clear their minds, and if you've ever sat in front of a campfire, you'll know how hypnotizing it can be. The same can be experienced with any type of open fire. Focus on the flames, the movements of the flame, the flickers. Even a minute of focus can help relax you.

Coloring/Painting

This is one of my personal favorites. My daughter can spend hours with a mandala or a canvas, and the personal satisfaction and calm she gets from the experience are abundantly clear. The quiet and inner peace from focusing on the colors, textures, and patterns provides the perfect opportunity to be calm and relax.

This experience is therapeutic beyond words. Painting and coloring have been, by far, my daughter's most successful experiences with mindfulness. She truly loses herself in the colors and brush strokes.

There are loads of free printables online and plenty of books to purchase on whatever takes your fancy. Or you could have a go at drawing yourself.

Reading

Another one of my personal favorites is reading. While in this case, you wouldn't be creating anything per se, you will be enjoying the creations of others. So, I strongly recommend choosing the right book for you. It doesn't have to be deep, scientific, or even an important piece of literature – it just has to be important to you. This way, you won't get bored, and your mind won't zone out to other thoughts. Pick a book you like, open the cover, and jump into your favorite world!

Try and read positive, inspirational books, and you will find they can motivate and improve your outlook. If you don't have time to read, how about an audiobook or podcast in the car, when traveling, or even as you relax in bed of an evening?

Music

Music is my escapism, and it is guaranteed to change my mood. Music can make you feel so much happier and calm, and it really is good for the soul. Whether it's on the radio in the car or while you are cleaning up, try and use music to help you relax. Choose pieces that will help you relax or ones you can sing along to that will lift your spirits. It is another creative method that you can employ in your meditation practice

Chapter 5 - Personal Touches

Using personal and sentimental touches can bring peace and happiness to you during your mindfulness meditation time. In this chapter, I will share two of my own personal practices where I use treasured items and my super-cute cat, Jasper.

Photographs of Family

Whenever I get time, I love to sit my children around me, find the family snaps, and start looking at old photos from our life or recent memories. Choose a few of your favorites and display them by your bed, or keep one with you in your bag. I have one on my bedside cabinet to remind me each night to be grateful for all I have.

This has turned into a soothing ritual for me on an evening, as I incorporate mindfulness most nights. I look at the photograph and run through all the wonderful things my children and family bring to my life, how precious they are, and how grateful I am. This little activity brings me such joy and peace and helps take away the stresses of the day (even if they have been little monkeys!).

Pets – Mindfulness with Pure Love

I am blessed to have a beautiful cat called Jasper, who is the best therapy for a stressed life. He is super-adorable and loves being stroked and brushed. If you have a pet (one that can be cuddled and stroked), both you and your furry friend can benefit from some relaxation time.

I love getting my kitty fix, and for a few minutes each day, it is lovely when my cat sits in my lap and starts purring.

During those moments, I don't even have to make an effort to clear my mind. I just sink into the soft and warm little furball sleeping peacefully in my lap, and I focus my entire mind on feeling the unconditional love. It is guaranteed to help you calm and reflect (and your pet will thank you too for the extra pampering).

Chapter 6 - Tips for a Happier You

Mindfulness meditation doesn't come with a magical guarantee that everything in life will be automatically right just because you start practicing it.

This is why you need to keep yourself grounded and find the right ways to make yourself happy.

In this chapter, I'm going to share a few tips that have helped me to stay happy or, at least, keep a positive outlook on life when things started to get on top of me. And let's face it, that can sometimes happen daily. As I am currently writing this during the COVID-19 pandemic, it is sometimes hard to keep upbeat with the constant doom and gloom in the media, the rising death rate, and the increase in positive test statistics. However, our view of the world and our approach to it can make a massive difference, help us keep the negative thoughts in the backs of our minds, and not let them impact our lives and how we are feeling.

Be Positive

Your outlook, the way you view different life events, has the strongest effect on your overall mood, how you react, and (much of the time) the outcome of most situations.

Once I understood this, I was able to slowly train myself to see the good and search for the silver lining in every unfortunate event I come across. I am not saying this is easy, but I have a written note on the front of my diary in big, bold writing:

This is good because...

My children groan when I repeat this back to them, but recently, my son conceded that he had used it when dealing with a difficult situation at school. It had made him feel much better about things. He probably regretted telling me this as I have mentioned it repeatedly ever since, but my point is that it does work!

Another example is that at the time of writing, my family is all in isolation. I tested positive for COVID-19 first, and then my husband also tested positive a few days later. Fourteen days inside, isolating and attempting to home-school while I was ill was not an appealing prospect. However, I re-wired my negative brain and ran through all the reasons this is good. I've had more time to spend with my children – my daughter has really improved her independent working skills and totally surprised me with her "can-do" attitude. My son has even learned how to actually put things in the dishwasher rather than leaving them on the bench for the dishwasher fairy to magically transport them for him.

However, the reality is, silver linings are not always an option. Sometimes it can just be too much. Sometimes, the clouds are just the beginning of a storm. At such times, I just remind myself that this too shall pass.

Difficulties in life are just our growing pains. They help us become better people and, once the storm has passed, we emerge as new, stronger versions of ourselves.

Be Kind

I am no saint. And it is bloody hard at times.

However, being positive and doing things for others makes you feel good.

Remembering a birthday, sending a text to someone to see how they are, bringing cake into work for no reason, or surprising someone with a coffee.

Sometimes it's just the little things. Sometimes it's just making time for someone to talk properly. Sometimes it's just listening properly, rather than giving superficial nods as I sometimes do when I really feel I don't have the time to listen.

The crux is, being kind will always come back to you, whether it's in positive karma points or just in the form of a good mood!

Spend Time with Those Who Matter

Time is so precious. We never know what's around the corner. Spend your time wisely; as we all know, it's hard to come by. Don't waste it with people who make you feel bad about yourself or do not offer any value to your life.

> *Think what and who really matters in your life and focus your energy there*

Make time to meet with friends and family and schedule it in. I know sometimes the effort is too much, and you can't be bothered and just want to snuggle up on the sofa. However, once you push yourself, it can provide an enormous boost to your wellbeing.

As my husband always reminds me (I had to include him in here at some point), nobody ever lay on their death bed and said, "I wish I had spent more time at work!" or "I really should have vacuumed more at home."

Think about what and who really matters in your life and focus your energy there

Conclusion

Well, I promised it would be a practical tool, and I hope you feel I've delivered.

I hope there are some elements you feel you can try and that you can adapt to suit your needs if you have not already.

Remember, the trick is to incorporate mindfulness and meditation into whatever you are doing already. It is impossible to list every opportunity, but my intention is to give some ideas about where it can work and inspire you to try it out.

Life throws lots of challenges at us, and there are many bumps along the way. It is just about how we deal with them. I promise mindfulness can make a difference.

I hope this has inspired you and has created a little more calm in your life.

Please spread the word if you feel this can help others, and check out my website www.happyandcalm.com

Bonus Goodies

Everyone loves a freebie!

I have personally seen the benefits of practicing meditation mindfulness, and I am passionate about helping where I can. On my website, I have added a contact form for you to get in touch and I will email some bonus tips and a printable sheet that will supplement the ideas in this book and help support you on your journey. So please check out www.happyandcalm.com for more details.